AF488839

IN THE BEGINNING...

SINCE THE DAWN OF TIME
THERE HAVE BEEN
OTHERS AMONG US.

THEY RESEMBLE US
IN MANY WAYS.
AND IN MANY
WAYS THEY
RESEMBLE US
NOT AT ALL.

YOU CAN IDENTIFY
THEM BY THEIR
STRANGE WALK
UNUSUAL CLOTHES
AND A CRAVING
FOR FLESH.

THEY ARE...

GAY PEOPLE
CROSS FIT

AND WHERE THERE ARE
GAY PEOPLE
THERE ARE BOUND TO BE....

GAY ZOMBIES!

TOM THE GAY ZOMBIE

IS

LIVING HIS

BEST AFTERLIFE

·YOU BETTER WORK·

AT THE OFFICE

KITCHEN ETIQUETTE

FLETCH

DROPS THE BALL

GETS STUCK IN OFFICE GOSSIP
AND THEN DAKOTA SAID...
DAMN YOU RIGOR MORTIS.
FLETCH

· OUT AND ABOUT ·

ZOMBEYONCÉ CONCERT

DECOM-POSE

CATEGORY IS... DROP DEAD GORGEOUS
10
10
10
HOUSE OF La MORTE
NECK CRACK
FAN CRACK
FLETCH

KILLER KARAOKE

WEEKEND PLANS
DRAG ME TO HELL
@ CLUBBED TO DEATH
SHEEZA MANEATER
DIDI DE LOS MUERTOS
SATURDAYS
MIDNITE
FLETCH

· GIRLS GOTTA EAT ·

LEAN CUISINE FOR LUNCH

SNACK BREAK

ZOMBIE FARMS
Alyssa Milanos
FLETCH

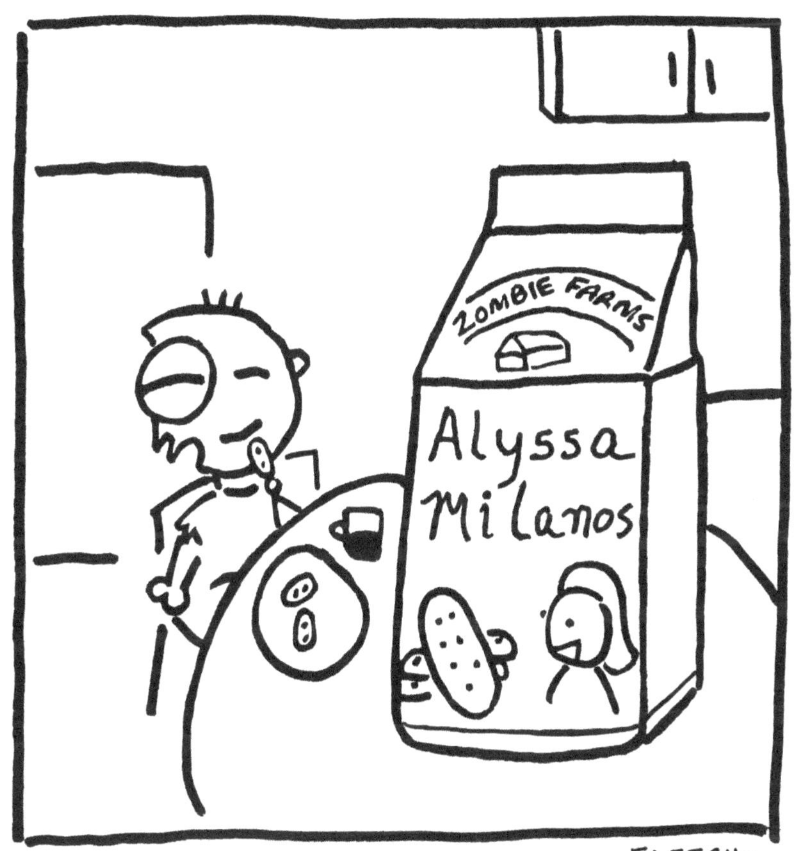

TRIES EATING VEGAN

BREAKFAST FOR DINNER

·GETS DROP DEAD GORGEOUS·

SAVING FACE

DEAD
SKIN
SCRUB
FLETCH

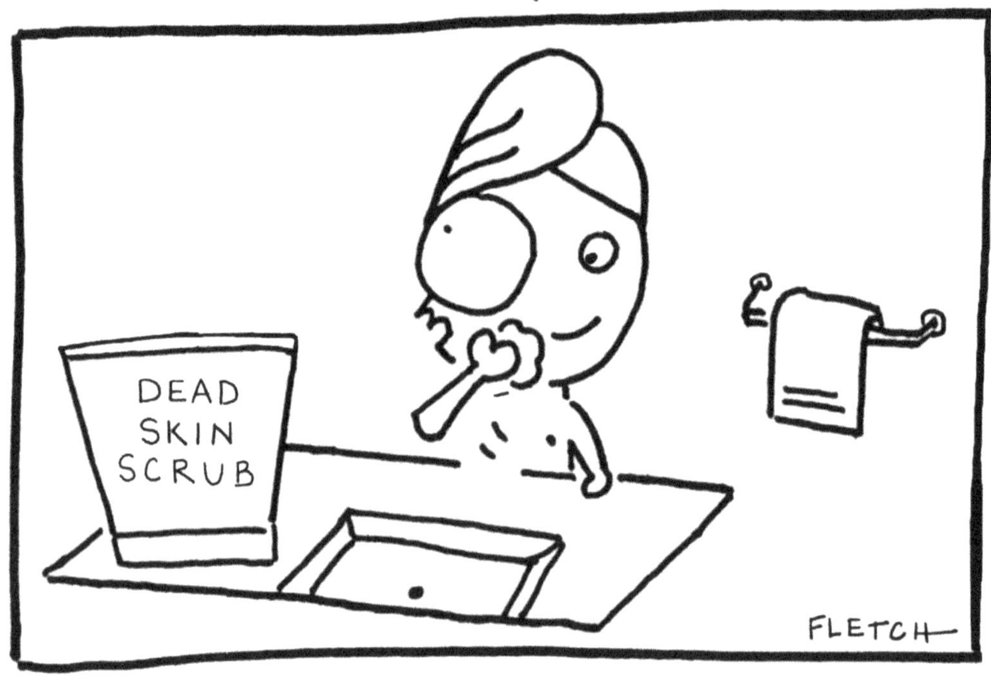

LIGHT WEIGHT

WHITENING APPOINTMENT

BARBIZOM MODELING SCHOOL

· THE STRUGGLE IS REAL ·

BUZZFEED

TOM
THE GAY
ZOMBIE
FLETCH

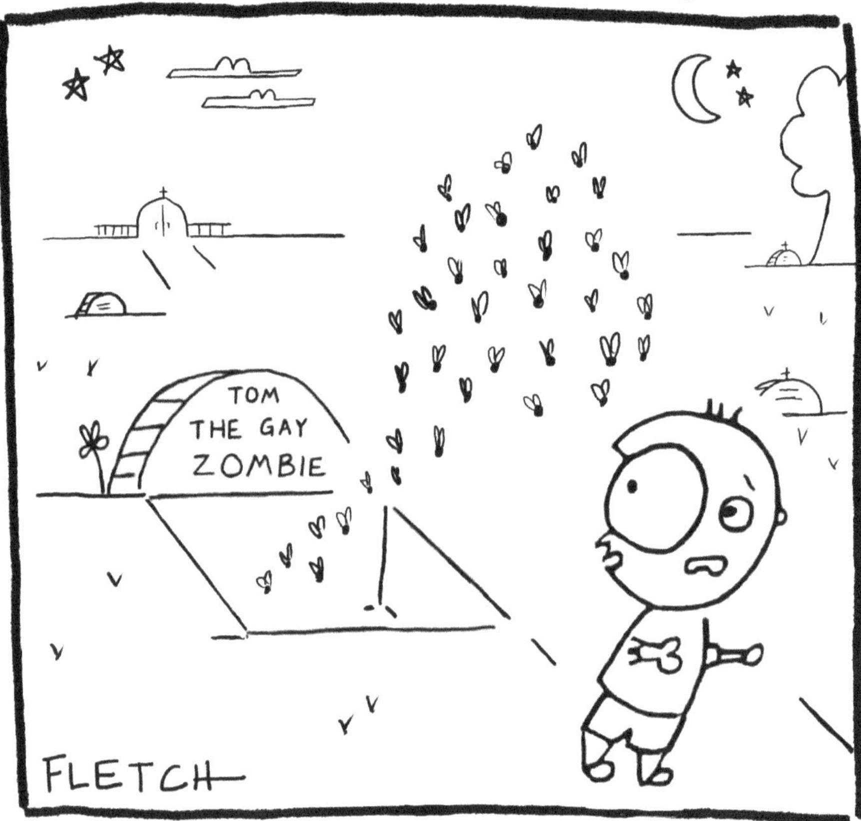

LOOKING FOR ZOM TOP

ZOM·BI·CURIOUS

INZOMNIA

COOLING
42
UNIZOM
I'LL
SLEEP
WHEN
I'M DEAD
A MEMOIR
FLETCH

· ZOMBIE'S BEST FRIEND ·

PUPPY TRAINING

FLETCH

CREATURE COMFORTS

THROW ME A BONE

· ME TIME ·

AFTER LIFE COACH

STAYING MINDFUL

MINDLESS READING

FLETCH

GUILTY PLEASURE

TOM THE GAY ZOMBIE

TOM THE GAY ZOMBIE

FLETCH IS A WRITER
AND ARTIST LIVING IN
MIAMI WITH HIS PARTNER
SERGIO AND THEIR
TINY DOG, PIERRE.

* 9 7 9 8 9 8 8 2 3 3 6 2 6 *